Advance Praise for

Gay Poetics of the Passion

Luis Lopez-Maldonado's *Gay Poetics of the Passion* combines the confessional with the devotional to delve deep, deeper than any other poet I have encountered, into his tumultuous life as a gay Chicano man in a homophobic society together with his Catholic upbringing within a pious family. The result is an invocation of identity brimming with passionate honesty and language that burns "like a volcanic rock" as it embraces the shockingly transgressive and in the process reinterprets and reaffirms his faith. Of special note is his sequence on the Stations of the Cross (the traditional 14 plus 4 of his own to boot) whose riveting retellings of Christ's Passion from a queer perspective—personal, political, theological—transform the profane and even the blasphemous into complex tapestries of reverence.

—**Orlando Ricardo Menes**, author of
The Gospel of Wildflowers and Weeds

Gay Poetics of the Passion is a blunt and unflinching journey by a young, gay Chicano. Intertwined with meditations on the divine and questions we press to our God in times of pain and betrayal, Maldonado's words dance along the cold, jagged edge between shame and reclamation. "I imagine there is nothing else in this world but this space," he writes, "but my heart thumping, my feet aching, my muscles flexing, and I believe in art once more…" Vulnerable and fierce, these poems explore a loneliness we must ultimately mold into something more for ourselves, if we are to survive it.

—**Michael Torres**

GAY POETICS OF THE PASSION

FLOWERSONG
P R E S S

poetry by

Luis Lopez-Maldonado

FLOWERSONG
PRESS

FlowerSong Press
Copyright © 2024 Edited by Luis Lopez-Maldonado
ISBN: 978-1-963245-11-0

Published by FlowerSong Press
in the United States of America.
www.flowersongpress.com

Cover Image by Melissa Artieda
Author Image Credit: Luis Lopez-Maldonado
Set in Adobe Garamond Pro

NOTICE: SCHOOLS AND BUSINESSES
FlowerSong Press offers copies of this book at quantity discount with bulk
purchase for educational, business, or sales promotional use. For information,
please email the Publisher at info@flowersongpress.com.

Proem

Happiness Makes *Mi* Empty

So stay the fuck away from *mí*. Today I hate the clouds & the rain & the sun is cold. My head is *pansona* with the faint smell of cow shit & Marlboros. My cock is hard & heavy, filled with milk & anxiety. Let them choke! Let them stare at my brownskin & point at my fading tattoos. I know this: tonight your forehead will be between my thighs & I will moan & hum sad songs. Don't forget to breathe! I see the night tonight paralyzing my hips, numbing my jaw, expanding the pupils on my dilated *ojos*. *Nombre del Padre, del Hijo, del Espíritu Santo... Mira güey*, I have never had love in *mí*, only fingers & fists & tongues & dicks, I've had Indians & Russians & Blacks, I think. I don't know anymore, I just know blood runs like silk out of *mí*. You see? If you look carefully, you will see happiness dissolving into nothingness. You will hear ravens talk. You will smell thousand-day-old *mecos* that linger inside *mí*. *Acercate.* Let me start over: smiling with crooked teeth, hair bleached & a fake nosering, works for me! Cummon let's pray. Is this normal, you think? *Amen.*

Dedication

For my parents who sacrificed their life in EL Granjenal, Michoacán (Mexico) so I could build mine in California and across the United States of America, for the many mujeres chingonas in my life, and for all my Latin@ LGBTQIA+ Raza, taking up well deserved space, wherever we go: Vivá!

Acknowledgements

I would like to thank everyone who read parts contained in this book, at one time or another. Thank you for your feedback, quierides friends, colleagues, and mentors. Gracias! The journey from start to finish of this project was both tiring and exhilarating. There were months when I wrote only one poem or prayer, and other times I couldn't stop writing. This piece of art has been marinating for 6 years, but I am eager to give it to you (no pun intended!), for now I am ready to let these poemitas exist among your hands and laps. I love you more than glitter. Cheers! One last thing: thank you to my haterz fan-club for being bullies, bigots, and bitches (some alliteration for you), for I am still here, still writing, still brown-queer, and I hope you love my second book of poemas; my next book will include poems about you.

table of contents

Proem v

Dedication vi

Acknowledgements vii

Stations Of The Cross 3

Personal History And Memory As It Plays In My Mind:
    Something Lost, Something\ Missing 25

Prayers: *Confesiones Del Alma* 61

Brown Boy Talks Queerness And Displacement In Amerika
    Or Flowers Bloom Even In Dry Grasses 81

About the Author 114

GAY POETICS OF THE PASSION

Stations Of The Cross

Opening Scream | Prayer—

O! My *Dios*, my redeemer, behold me here at Thy feet, *tus pies limpios.*
From the bottom of my brown ♥: I am sorry for all my sins. If by them I
have offended TheeThyThou, who art infinitely good *y hermoso*, I would
rather die commit suicide & say goodbye than offend Thee again, my Lord.
~~Gaymen~~ Amen.

I.

First Station | *Jesus* is condemned to death

Nooooo one spoke ↑ for you
defended you
loved you back the way you did
because you didn't ask for help
or you knew we wouldn't,
it doesn't really matter.
Crimson draping
over white cotton
silky blond coffee hair
dark beard dark mustache,
your eyes I don't remember.
But we stood still
as they wrapped your large hands
with wet rope,
the one they use on horses & mules
& they pushed you
from behind (I like it from behind)
calling you King! & *Jesús de Nazarete*!
Your long eyelashes lifting
up & down up & down
your eyes trying to find
another set of eyes
to lock with:
no luck. Roses cut
stems made into art
a crown of thorns smashed
upon your head & face

a smirk on the soldier's face
as he pulled you
from behind him, like cattle.
Fuck. Where is your my God, now?

II.
Second Station | *Jesus* carries His cross

Blood dripped from your face like broken faucets &
    a heavy wooden cross was thrown over your shoulders &

back & spine. Women screamed screeched like cats,
    men with hands over their mouth looking down

to the pale ground. Clouds began to gather.

    You walk, chin up chest up &
pass faces that once kissed your cheek feet seat,

    Your dry mouth opens & in the distance
a silent thank you escapes Mary a mile away,

    black *rebozo* over her hair, right hand over her ♥,
a sudden loss of breath. Women screamed. Children cried.

    Soldiers smiled with crooked teeth. (I took a #selfie)
Wild flowers went limp like exhausted cocks &
    it begins|began|begun…

III.
Third Station | *Jesus* falls for the first time

Horses scratch their hoofs. People stand & watch you walk by.
You fall. The wooden † hits the floor. The earth shakes.

The sun burns through your dark eyes dark hair
bloody face, your cracked lips open in a silent scream for help:

Where are you Father? Appá?
Men in leather armor laugh at you whip you

tell you to get your ass up & stop being a little bitch.
Get up. Get up. The frozen women on the side roads

covering their faces with cotton shawls short nails pale stares.
Somewhere in the distance: two more †s are being shaped

hammered washed, holes being dug, prisoners laughing
at the guards busting a sweat. Your thighs tremble as you get up.

They throw the † over your shoulder, again.

IV.
Fourth Station | *Jesus* meets his mother

Clouds
gather in
the sky &
blue turns to grey.
Your tired eyes scan
the crowd in search of something
more than hypocrites & paparazzi
(I have been called both) She squints her light eyes,
irritated from crying. Her milk skin is dirty & embarrassed.
She suffers. She weeps. She walks up to the †, ♥ sinking
down to her covered toes, tears to mucus to mouth. You reach
out to her & grab her by the elbow, she weeps, tells you my son my son
& the guards whip you. **Whip!** She screams; more tears. **Whip! Whip! Whip!**
O! Dear.

V.
Fifth Station | Simon of Cyrene helps *Jesus* to carry his cross

Blisters pulse on your feet, you can't see out of your right eye anymore
too much blood too much love. You walk slowly as if your ribs are already crushed
& your hips frozen, the ✝ falls & you begin to drag it
(I've been dragged and gagged too). You are slow. The sun is scorching.

The guards yell at you whip you & you move like a turtle still.
A thick man gets pushed & shoved to the ✝. They make him help you
carry the ✝ because you are taking too long man, because it's hot they're hungry
& the other two prisoners are already being nailed to their ✝s.

They squirm like little girls. We have to hurry this shit up. Go! Walk!
You put your head down staring at the dust,
muttering to *Dios*. Somewhere in the distance the cries of your mother
continue (moms can be annoying, I know) her eyes puffy with despair,
her hands vibrating shaking like yours.

VI.

Sixth Station | Veronica wipes the face of *Jesus*

It's warm. All you hear are screams
from the crowd. You grind your red teeth
try to swallow but your throat is not working anymore.
(Swallowing ain't easy ya know, takes practice, Ha!)
More blood drips from your head. Go! Walk!
They continue to whip your ass
in search of something more than just a fall.
Because you keep falling failing to carry your †.
(You failed me many times when I cried for help)

Her name is *Veronica*. She appears from nowhere
& approaches you. Her kind eyes feed your soul.
(Yes cliché, I know)
She hands you a cloth & helps you wipe your face
so that you can see. They say your face came off.
That your fucked up reflection stayed on the cloth
as she pulled it away from your face. I didn't see.
That your blessing stayed between her hands
milk hands that reminded you of *tu ama*
sweet & delicate & pure.   Move! Another whip.

More screams. Dry throat. Broken ♥. (Join the club boo)

VII.
Seventh Station | *Jesus* falls the second time

Whip! Whip! Whip!   Get up.

You must keep going you must die today for all these fucking sinners
around you for the future rapists & drug dealers

      (For that white guy that fucked me at 17)

                keep walking to your death
      for all those who do not believe in your father.

You   fall again. Fall #2.   It seems like you have fallen 100x

      that your bones are slowly breaking
            your eyes too red to be eyes
                  & your crown of thorns,

          heavier.

You get back up.   **Whip!**   A silent scream for help.   **Whip!**

      Head down,
      † on shoulder,
      horses surround you.

Dirt.

      Blood.

          Sweat.   Clouds begin to gather.

VIII.

Eighth Station | *Jesus* meets the woman of Jerusalem

How many more stations?
You look like shit.
(Just being honest dude)
I am sure you feel like shit.
But you stop to help a baby crying.
Several women with upside-down smiles.
Whip!
They keep whipping you
Harassing you
Laughing at your royal crown.
But you don't move.
You reach your hands & encourage them.
(I could never do that)
Try to smile at them
With them
& you look up to the heavens.
The sky is empty.
Flooded with clouds.
The sun slowly fading.
Your ♥ full.
You bow your head.
Maybe out of respect.
Or maybe because you are so fucking tired.
Your feet are numb.
You pee on yourself.
Whip!

IX.

Ninth Station | *Jesus* falls a third time

Fall number three. Really? Don't they see you can't walk anymore!
Can't they see the ribs sticking out from your chest & stomach?

Stop! Leave him the fuck alone! You lifeless pieces of shit!
You are killing the sun of God! You are killing us all!

You're almost done, *ya mero.* You fall. You take a deep breath.
In the distance: On a hill, two wooden †s.

The middle spot, empty. Because you know that one is for you,
for the † you carry through & through the town, for the freak-show

you are about to put on. More clouds. Thunder. Lightning. Laughs.

Whip!

You scream up to the grey sky & get up, again.
You get up (mad respect to you hunny)

X.
Tenth Station | *Jesus* clothes are taken away

Your limp cock hangs like ripe bananas,

(Now I'm hungry)

your overgrown curls cascade down your balls

like spiderwebs & they continue to laugh at you.

"You are the King! Are you not? Do a miracle!"

Whip! The blood-covered cloak hugs your feet now.

The sun is dead. (I feel dead) The clouds are alive.

Screaming. Like your mother. You seem to stare at the sky

in search of a butterfly or a bee, but you see nothing,

everything; the crowds tease you.

You are alone. You are naked. You are done.

A subtle smile tattooed on your chiseled face.

(How many more tattoos must I get

to feel the pain that compares to yours?)

XI.
Eleventh Station | *Jesus* is nailed to the cross

Nails puncture hands & feet
blood oozing like raspberry syrup:
in the distance there
is rain there is thunder
& your mother faints.
♥ stops.

You are now stretched on your †.
Black crows circle the mountain
where two †s stand.
Your ribs exposed *tus huevos* too,
your breath stinking of innocence.
(How does that smell though?)

Soldiers laugh
& spit on your frozen body.
Frozen eyes pale face cracked lips.
No one fucking cared no one fucking listened
no one fucking cared no one gave a rats-ass
if you were the son of God:
some fucked-up shit *Jesus*
(Bullshit if you ask me!)

Clouds flood the sky.
Rain begins to fall. Thunder. Lighting.

XII.
Twelfth Station | *Jesus* dies on the cross

Jesus, there you hang on the ✝ like a solo overripe *mango*
it doesn't matter anymore dude, you are ~~through~~. Your thorn
crown tops your body like a cherry on an ice cream Sunday,
your ribs exposed, mouth half-open or half-closed, I can't tell.
Your mother screams (Fuck, she screams a lot) Other screams.
The men cover their mouths, *pinches putos.* Lighting! Thunder!
Rain. Next: you die. More screams. Blood drips from ankles
& *Magdalena* kisses them; she looks like a whore on all fours
(I've been there) ~~blood~~ lipstick all over her face. Still no miracle,
no God up above no *Jésus de Nazareth.* I am a bit disappointed.
Show's over. (Can we get our $ back?)

XIII.

Thirteenth Station | The body of *Jesus* is taken down from the cross

They drop your body on Mary's lap.
    She begins to weep. Hands wipe your body,
        dirt-covered clothes blood-soaked shawls,
           the bloody crown softly removed
                as if it were made of rose petals. The rain becomes angry.

       ♥'s across the nation world galaxy are broken.

       Guards disappear. The two other criminals left behind
     to rot, their ✝s still upright stained with guilty sweat
  & blood. Rain. Rain. Rain. Mary kisses your forehead
 (I would have kissed your eyes, mouth, and hips too):
"You are free. My son! You are free."

XIV.

Fourteenth Station | *Jesus* is laid in the tomb

This is it homie, the last of the epic stations
the moment where every Catholic
prays a Hail Mary & thinks they know
the rest of the story;
those bitches
don't know shit
don't know that you didn't
take 3 days to wake up
that you did not die for them
but because of them! *Pendejos!*
(myself included).

They put a large stone to protect your body
like someone is going to want to steel it
& freeze your eyeballs or something.
(Let's be honest, you aren't Michael Jackson)

You are forgotten within days.
"Followers of Christ" until you die
& then they go back to gambling in temples
putting their hands up women's skirts (my skirt!)
steeling $$$ from the poor: Hypocrites.

XV.
Fifteen Station | God™ watches *Jesus* resurrect

My son sunrise rise from the dark from the mud tomb you're stuck in
from the hole these humans have put you in
from the holes they have drilled in
your holy skin in in in,
I am here now hijo, I AM here and there and everywhere
your brown curls dry like a desert
eyes of honey teeth of pearls
the ways your nude thighs glisten listen to the songs of birds
celebrating your resurrection: *RISE!*

Open your arms & eyes & mouth & soul
let those in need come to their knees needs
smile when you hear my name your name our name
& build an army of love of water of earth,
Say to them this: *Al que quede vencedor le otorgaré que se siente conmigo en mi trono,
como también you vencí, y me senté con mi Padre en su trono.*

XVI.

Sixteenth Station | *Jesus* visits his friends and appears to the people

XVII.

Seventeenth Station | *Jesus* is not home, *no en casa*

You lie.
I call for you
& you don't cum
you don't stop my cousin
from shooting himself in the head,
you don't stop the cancer
eating my Godmother's
liver & throat & lungs,
you don't stop Trump from winning
& making Amerikkka whiter.
& you don't come.
But I keep
praying.
You lie.

You lie.
Knocks on your door
& you make it rain
you give us an extra day
in February,
you send
the groundhog|spring early,
you put a woman
against a man
for presidency.
But what about *mi?*

What about my knocking?

XVIII.
~~Eighteenth~~ Station | Advice for the face of God™

Here is a helpful guide for
Catholic Priests everywhere:
GAY HANKY-PANKY CODE
Black is heavy top | heavy bottom!
Grey is bondage top | I want to be tied!
Light Blue wants head | cocksucker!
Teal Blue is a cock & ball torturer | torture!
Red means you are a fist-fucker | fist fuckee!
Light Pink has dildos | fuck me, fuck me!
Lavender likes queens | I'm a dragqueen!
Tiffany Green only fucks children | fuck my tight son!
Yellow loves to piss | piss freak!
Mustard means you have a huge cock | I want 8" +
Orange is bad like Satan | anything anytime now!
Olive Drab is a military top | military bottombitch!
Beige dives tongue in butthole | toss my salad!
Brown Lace is being uncut | I fucking love uncut!
Brown Satin is being cut | I'll pass on the cut cock!
Cream means you cum in condoms | I swallow from condom!
White w/Multicolor Dots is hosting an orgy | looking for an orgy!
Red w/Rosary is ass beads | rip my hole apart!

Personal History And Memory As It Plays In My Mind: Something Lost, Something Missing

His room as I recall: White walls. Queen-sized bed. Candles lit. Box of condoms on top of dresser. The bathroom door slightly open, light turned on. Tan carpet. 20 lb. weights on floor next to some running shoes, Nikes or Adidas, I don't remember. Some Marlboro's and a lighter on top of a dark bookshelf. Hardly any books but the bible dead center.   I didn't know what to do. How to sit. If I should talk or if I should take my shoes off and start undressing myself.   I was lost. A scared virgin. A gay guy about to bloom. My first time (cliché, yes I know). My first shot at being gay. Whatever that means…

"If a man practices homosexuality, having sex with another man as with a woman, both men have committed a detestable act. They must both be put to death, for they are guilty of a capital offense."
                              —Leviticus 20:13

(**Directions:** Light a cigarette as you read this poem)

I lost count after the first month of fucking around. I remember specific times, cities, faces, but that's it; I have no idea how many times I gave my body away. How many times they took what they wanted and left me unconscious. Drunk. Beat-up. If I would have to guess to save me life, I would say this: From 2003-2009 to be fair and round up, I had sex once a week— at times I was having sex 5 or 6 times a week with different men— with over 200 different men. Penetrated = over 700 times? Too much math. So many flavors to choose from. So little time…

"Do not practice homosexuality, having sex with another man as with a woman. It is a detestable sin."
                                        —Leviticus 18:22

I became a slut right out of high school, some gays would probably say; college was a forced push for me to begin blooming. So what better way to start fresh than by painting over my vomit blue room. Right?   I grew up hating blue because it was a color chosen for *mí*, blue was for boys. But I was not the same as every other boy. I was different. So I deserved a different color, dammit!

"That is why God abandoned them to their shameful desires. ████

████████████████ men, instead of having normal sexual relations with women, burned with lust for each other. Men did shameful things with other men, and as a result of this sin, they suffered within themselves the penalty they deserved. Since they thought it foolish to acknowledge God, he abandoned them █████

—Romans 1: 26-28

I was enjoying life at this point. I was 18. I was making money. I was fucking customers | businessclients. Thanks Bank of America™. I was having fun. I was making money $$$$$$ ...

"And don't forget Sodom and Gomorrah and their neighboring towns, which were filled with immorality and every kind of sexual perversion. Those cities were destroyed by fire and serve as a warning of the eternal fire of God's judgment."
—Jude 1:7

School. Work. Come home late. Lights off. Another date. Another fuck. Another mistake. School. Work. Come home late from date. Text from "my regular | fuck buddy."   Another Fuck. Another day…

"But Peter and the apostles replied, "We must obey God rather than any human authority."
                    —Acts 5:29

I stare at my green walls now, poetry books stacked in the corner of the room by the large window, my dance bags on the floor next to my yoga mat, crosses hanging everywhere— I collect them— and a worn-out Mickey Mouse tucked somewhere below my comforter, full of cum and regrets. Cum and regrets. Lots of cum…

"So I say, let the Holy Spirit guide your lives. Then you won't be doing what your sinful nature craves. The sinful nature wants to do evil,

Let me tell you again, as I have before, that anyone living that sort of life will not inherit the Kingdom of God."
—Galatians 5:16-21

Every morning when I get up it feels like déjà vu, the same thing over and over again. As soon as I get out of bed to reach for my cell phone or turn the alarm clock off, my body cracks in six different places. Roll my neck roll my neck curve down and uncurl, one vertebrae at a time. I am not twenty-one anymore...

"But cowards, unbelievers, the corrupt, murderers, the immoral, those who practice witchcraft, idol worshipers, and all liars— their fate is in the fiery lake of burning sulfur. This is the second death."
                                        —Revelation 21:8

My family has never really been there for me, I got used to it, and I became numb to it too...

"While they were enjoying themselves, a crowd of troublemakers from the town surrounded the house. They began beating at the door and shouting to the old man, 'Bring out the man who is staying with you so we can have sex with him.'"

—Judges 19:22

Once my grandfathers died, everything seemed to slowly fall apart. Aunts and uncles started getting into fights. Cousins stopped calling eachother cousins. Respect was no where to be found...

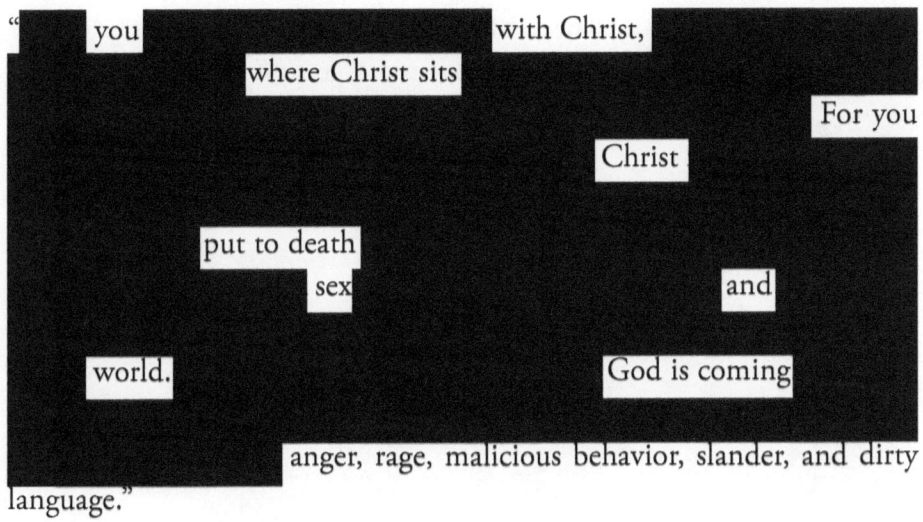

"   you   with Christ,
              where Christ sits
                                                      For you
                                      Christ

      put to death
              sex   and

      world.   God is coming

anger, rage, malicious behavior, slander, and dirty language."

—Colossians 3:1-8

They all have light skin, I am dark, *moreno*. They have curly hair, I have straight hair, *pelo lasio*. They eat meat, I used to eat meat. They are weak. I have never been...

"God alone, who gave the law, is the Judge. He alone has the power to save or to destroy. So what right do you have to judge your neighbor?"
—James 4:12

They know nothing. Yet. They don't care. And my father, my father really doesn't care for anyone! But for himself. He stopped being a man manymany years ago, after he died in 1990. He came back to life though…

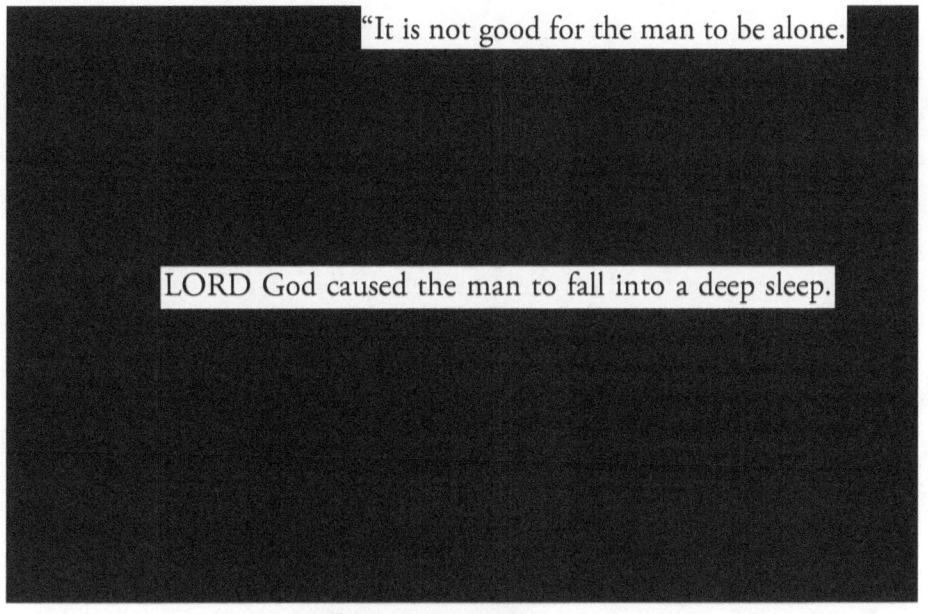

"It is not good for the man to be alone.

LORD God caused the man to fall into a deep sleep.

—Genesis 2:18-25

He died on a Monday morning. Work. Construction site. No hard-hat. Three floors. A large piece of cement fell on him, crushed his skull, ripped off his face, and took away his masculinity— a human vegetable. They pronounced him dead that same night, there was nothing they could do, he was destroyed. Horrific accident? Nine-hour surgery, a hundred tubes | snakes coming out from his patched body: a monster! He lay dead on the bed surrounded by his wife and mother, sisters and brothers coming in and out, his children at home, no clue at all. He began breathing after thirty minutes, his chest lifting the white sheets upanddown, upanddown. A miracle.   He is a miracle baby. He was born again, given a second chance, a second birthday. I'm technically older than he is…

"For from the heart come evil thoughts, murder, adultery, all sexual immorality, theft, lying, and slander."
                    —Mathew 15:19

My mother: this woman has suffered. Kindergarten dropout. At age seven she becomes responsible for things usually tied with thirty year olds: Raise ten kids. Walks countless miles to fetch clean water, to wash clothes, to sell *pan dulce* my grandfather and uncle make. Goes to bed hungry five days a week. Kids need to eat…

She is more precious than rubies.

She is energetic and strong, a hard worker. Her

hands are busy spinning thread, her fingers twisting fiber.

—Proverbs 31:10-20

School. Work. Come home late. Lights off. Another date. Another fuck. Another mistake.

Now my room feels like a home when I come home late from a movie or show or a small get together— a dinner with the girls, a night at the Abbey on Santa Monica Blvd, a family party at my boyfriend's place. Now-a-days not as late though. I stare at my green walls now, poetry books stacked in the corner of the room by the large window, my dance bags on the floor next to my yoga mat, crosses hanging everywhere— I collect them — and a worn-out Mickey Mouse tucked somewhere below my comforter. And the green walls now become black once again, but this time just through the night. I sometimes lay staring up at nothing, thinking of everything around me, inside me, and praying to God for the day and for the next one I will wake to.

I love being alone. There is something mysteriously arousing about sleeping alone, I mean I love to wake up to smooth skin that is not mine, of course, who doesn't, but there is something about being alone, sleeping alone, waking up alone, that excites me! The reflection of the moon sometimes sneaks in, and I think about how we are all connected, how life manages to be the same everywhere, how the dead also live, how no matter how small we think we are comparing to nature and the size of our world, that we still matter and have a role— there is someone like me or exactly like me somewhere else in this world... there has got to be...

"You must abstain from eating food offered to idols, from consuming blood or the meat of strangled animals, and from sexual immorality. If you do this, you will do well. Farewell."
—Acts 15:29

Name: ████████████████

"Real" Full Name: ██████████████████████

Age: I always say I'm younger than I am, at least by two years; so 28

Height: 6'0" or 6"1 (doesn't matter)

Latino/Mexican (mixed, exotic, spanish)

"Fools think their own way is right, but the wise listen to others."
—Proverbs 12:15

Versatile|Vers: This usually means that you are able to give and receive, to top or bottom, to be passive|submissive and active|aggressive etc…

Uncut|Uc: This refers to your penis; I am ███████████████████

Smooth: My body is smoother than hairier. I have little to no hair. Soft skin.

Hung: My █████████████████ inches. Thick…

GL: Good Looking

NSA: No Strings Attached

Clean: HIV ████████

"Outside the city are the dogs--the sorcerers, the sexually immoral, the murderers, the idol worshipers, and all who love to live a lie."
—Revelation 22:15

Travel: This means that I cannot host, have you over at my place, but rather travel, I can go to you. That sound good?

Poppers/PNP: These are used to alleviate the pain in anal sex and to increase sexual arousal. These are considered recreational drugs. I do not use these but do not mind if you do. Drugs, party and play, are usually not in my repertoire but I am not against them. You call the shots if you are hung and hot.

DL: Down low; discrete

Bareback|BB: Sex is amazing bareback! This is known when a condom is not used in anal sex or blowjobs. Everyone is at risk. It's just smarter to use condoms. I never got tested, always lied, bareback is all I wanted, all I got. Now, *sexo* with strangers must involve a condom. No condom, get the fuck out of here...

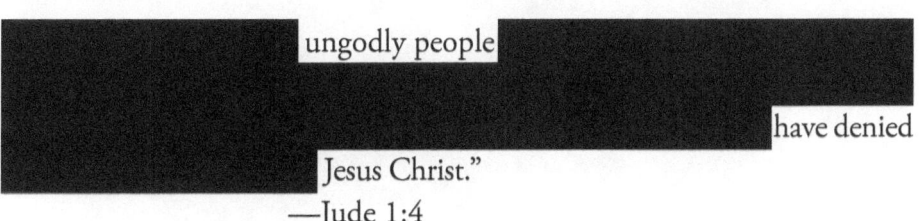

"ungodly people have denied Jesus Christ."
—Jude 1:4

Sexual Fantasy: Fuck a priest. Maybe inside a church or in the confessional room! Rosary beads included, please. (This already happened. Thanks Notre Dame® ☺ and Grindr ☺)

"...the triumph of the wicked has been short lived and the joy of the godless has been only temporary?"
—Job 20:5

In our e-mails he asked me what I wanted to do and I told him; some lies and some truth. I told him I was a virgin and that I had never done anything with a guy before. This was true but I did lie about my age. I said I was 23 when I was really 17. Rape? I don't think it matters anymore. I can't remember a face or a name and besides, he was in town for business…

"Let the one who is doing harm continue to do harm; let the one who is vile continue to be vile; let the one who is righteous continue to live righteously; let the one who is holy continue to be holy. Look, I am coming soon, bringing my reward with me to repay all people according to their deeds."

—Revelation 22:11-12

I knew I was gay. I knew my parents thought my kind were bad, a sin. But I knew I was smart. I knew I was gay…

"Their minds are full

—Ephesians 4:18-19

Every morning when I get up it feels like déjà vu, the same thing over and over again. As soon as I get off my bed, to reach for my cell phone or turn the alarm clock off, my body cracks in six different places. I am getting closer to my mid-thirties, I think to myself. In reality, I am only twenty-nine or thirty but I feel like forty-four sometimes…

"And he has given us this command: Those who love God must also love their Christian brothers and sisters."
—John 4:21

I had never been exposed to something like this in my life, not because my family could not afford it, but because they did not know of it themselves— they only knew of their culture and traditions, soccer, *musica Ranchera/Banda/Mariachi,* church on Sundays, *pozole* for Christmas™, *tamales* for Thanksgiving™. So I am a bit disappointed in them for that, for not knowing anything about my culture, for not allowing their children to choose what they wanted to do. I had to discover my passion on my own and it was too late. I was 17! This is a red flag, a no-no, you do not begin your piano lessons this late in your life, or your ballet classes, or your singing classes etc… you just don't.   But I did…

"For from within, out of a person's heart, come evil thoughts, sexual immorality, theft, murder, adultery, greed, wickedness, deceit, lustful desires, envy, slander, pride, and foolishness."
—Mark 7:21-22

I sometimes close my eyes before the curtain goes up and lose I myself in the black space— an empty heaven for me.

I begin to hear every light cue, feel every bump on the marley floors, smell every piece of duct tape used to hold down the extension cords.

I imagine there is nothing else in this world but this space, but my heart thumping, my feet aching, my muscles flexing, and I believe in art once more...

"Whoever stubbornly refuses to accept criticism will suddenly be destroyed beyond recovery."
                    —Proverbs 29:1

Once my grandfathers died, everything seemed to slowly fall apart. Some aunts and uncles did not talk to each other because of misunderstandings or minor fights, cousins stopped being cousins, family stopped caring. Kids don't even play anymore!

They don't know what playing outside means, playing baseball, handball, dodge ball. My cousins now sit in corners with their iPads or Gameboys, sometimes don't even

say hi...

"A fool is quick-tempered, but a wise person stays calm when insulted."
—Proverbs 12:16

I am nothing like them. Of them. To them.

They all have light skin, I am dark, *moreno*. They have curly hair, I have straight hair, *pelo lasio*.

"...so ignore them. They are blind guides leading the blind, and if one blind person guides another, they will both fall into a ditch."
    —Mathew 15:14

At fifteen he came with his father to California from Mexico, began working the strawberry and the orange. He went back and forth for years. He met mom and married her when she was sixteen, he was eighteen. Eighteen.

"God blesses those who are persecuted for doing right, for the Kingdom of Heaven is theirs. God blesses you when people mock you and persecute you and lie about you and say all sorts of evil things against you because you are my followers."

—Mathew 5:10-11

At nineteen he was a father. At twenty-three he bought a house. At twenty-four he was a father of four, two boys, two girls.

"Read Whatever verse you want."

He is the biggest case in the history of the City of Santa Ana; proof hangs on the marble walls of the federal building.

He made his lawyer a millionaire ☑

He stopped loving his wife, stopped living for others, takes pills every day, injects himself with insulin, takes his handicap card everywhere he is driven, is legally blind, lost sensation of taste, takes a shit ten minutes after he eats, pisses every hour. But everyone loves him! Everyone asks for him, for $$$, wants to talk to him, hangout with him, play pool with him.

He used to be a man, the best soccer player in the leagues, a chick-magnet, blue eyes, thick hair, lean body. He used to be…

"Read: Open the bible at random, and point and read."

At fifteen a virus fucked her over, and ignorant dentists had to pull out all her teeth, left her broken-hearted. Fake teeth went in! A year later she married and got pregnant before she was seventeen...

"Don't read a verse after this poem." –

Bled to death from my brother. Stitches. Both her breasts infested with puss and enlarged three times their normal size...

"The LORD has made everything for his own purposes, ████████ ████████████████

—Proverbs 16:4

C-section gave her trauma and gifted her with a four-month anemia. Her husband kept drinking and filled her once more. I was not supposed to happen. Doctors said I wouldn't live; I was four weeks over-due, forced to come-out, eyes of blood, didn't cry from spanks, couldn't breathe on my own. My mother's breasts were infected and had to go under the knife...

"Do not drag me away with the wicked--with those who do evil--those who speak friendly words to their neighbors while planning evil in their hearts."

—Psalm 28:3

I was never fed breast milk. They had dried before I was born...

"Everyone who sees me mocks me.

LORD save him!

trust you at my mother's breast."

—Psalm 22:7-9

Her teeth are replaced every five years. Her stomach suffers from ulcers. Migraines attack her through out the year; doctors ordered her to stop driving. She dreams weird-ass shit, and within days, there is a family death or some other cursed disease. Priests told her to embrace her gift. Appendix had to come out. Menopause just paid her a visit and is here to stay...

"Your kindness will reward you, but your cruelty will destroy you."
—Proverbs 11:17

Prayers: *Confesiones Del Alma*

The Virgin Mary,

For those of us who are killed and dismembered for being gay. For those men attacked in restaurants | on the streets. For the gay couple that will be beat next week in Texas or Oklahoma. For the queer in all of us. Pray for us. *Ruega por nosotros.*

The Blessed Virgin,

For safe anal sex. Say no to bb bareback! Pray for us. *Ruega por nosotros.*

The Blessed Virgin Mary,

For all Transgender Women or Men. To keep them safe away from bullies and homophobic "religious" people. For those that I called friends, whose wigs were covered in blood, heels spread across asphalt, faces smashed against brick walls.
RIP Katya De La Riva. Pray for us. *Ruega por nosotros.*

The Holy Virgin,

For the innocent who are raped and beaten. For the blood dripping down tender thighs and feet. For forced prostitution all over the world. Pray for us. *Ruega por nosotros.*

The Virgin,

For the gay lost souls stuck still on earth. For those murdered with words in their mouths. For those burned alive. For those who couldn't scream before they hung from rope. Pray for us. *Ruega por nosotros.*

The Virgin Mother,

For all those damn Drag Queens and Kings. For their flamboyant outfits and rhinestoned panty-hose. For their comedy and silly fucked-up jokes. Thanks for making us me smile, time and time again. Pray for us. *Ruega por nosotros.*

Saint Mary,

For those of us who swallow. For those that have to swallow, to stay clean and leave no suspicious residue behind. For those that can't afford a teeth-whitening procedure. Pray for us. *Ruega por nosotros.*

Holy Mary,

For all the underage teens who lie to get fucked too soon by who knows who. For those that were fucked without consent. For the troubled gay youth that suck'n'fuck for some $. For those who fuck up their lives with drugs and sex. Pray for us. *Ruega por nosotros*.

Mary Mother of Jesus,

For those who are bullied in school for being different, bullied for being weird, bullied for being HIV + bullied for being fat, bullied for being gay, bullied for being poor, bullied for being brown | black | yellow | green | red, bullied for being late to class, bullied for being short bullied for being them. Pray for us. *Ruega por nosotros.*

The Blessed Mother,

For those LGBTQ supporters and advocates, so they could continue defending us against ignorant people who claim we are confused and a joke. For those forced by church to undergo bullshit reverse-psychology gay banning treatments. For all those kicked-out from their homes because their stupid-ass parents think they are no longer blood-related. Pray for us. *Ruega por nosotros.*

The Holy Mother,

For those who don't have the balls to come-out and are scared to death for being fabulous and glittery. Pray for us. *Ruega por nosotros.*

The Mother Of God,

For those who are denied marriage licenses, still; fuck that! Bullshit. For those not hired, for looking | sounding gay. For those getting paid too little. For those discriminated against at restaurants department stores church. For those laughed at, fingers pointed to hair chest crotch shoes. Pray for us. *Ruega por nosotros.*

Mary Mother Of God,

For all the streetwalkers, whore shoppers, those that polish cocks in cars so they can feed their children and pay the rent. Pray for us. *Ruega por nosotros.*

The Madonna,

For those who feel they are unnatural and guilty and wrong and bad and ugly. Please give them strength, protect them from wrong-doing, from trying to hang themselves, cut themselves, drown themselves, from trying to punish their souls. Pray for us. *Ruega por nosotros.*

Our Lady,

For those who lose the battle to fame, to insecurity, to curiosity, to child-porn, to incest, to HIV, to cocaine, to peer pressure. For those in denial. For those who hide. Pray for us. *Ruega por nosotros.*

Our Blessed Lady,

For the entire Trump | Hitler supporters. For the white racists bigots tearing our people apart, tearing the stars off our American flag. Pray for us. *Ruega por nosotros.*

Our Lady Of Good Success,

For those stuck in the in-between, soul in hand, heart lost in the abyss. For those that linger the earth in search of God and forgiveness. For those who are willing to forgive. Pray for us. *Ruega por nosotros.*

Our Lady Of Mount Carmel,

For the recent KKK revival in Orange County, CA. For the black girl getting kicked out of a Trump rally, pushed and punched along the way. For the whole world who watches the United States of America with fear and sadness during the presidential election. Pray for us. *Ruega por nosotros.*

Brown Boy Talks Queerness
And Displacement In Amerika Or
Flowers Bloom Even In Dry Grasses

1

After the conquest, my people were landless. Old ~~California~~ *Mejico* looked nothing like it does today. Telephone posts lined like wooden crosses, one after another, signs of life for the Mexicans that rode on horses traveling back to an unknown home—

equality   only a speck of dead light up in the blurred sky.

2

Christopher Columbus lied. You can't discover something that is already here, flowers blooming in the spring, seagulls lounging around by the tide, the sky burning blue into this clear-night October California air. I stare glare out & listen to the wind, rushing ocean waves— spindrift rising, whispers of the Indigenous people who were here when the white man came, yelling & screaming with guns in hand.

3

One night the Four Angels of Light paid me a visit, myroom dark, suffocating, the heat rising from downstairs in the summer time. My body was held down, pinned to my bed in an open position, like how Jesus was nailed drilled to the wooden cross. On the outskirt of my throat something burned, my silent screams ignored, my browneyes frozen ceiling. I don't move— the absence of light swallows my existence beyond

these four walls.

4

My *prima Maricruz* says no. He rapes her. She kills him. She calls me. I pick her up. I am the only one who believes her. I call her in jail. I sit across from her pale face, her over-tweezed eyebrows, her glossy black hair, the stink of drunk on her breath. She stares through *mí*, beyond my poetess mind & I don't know what she seeks for:

Silencio. Even the birds outside are mute. Time is up! I stand to leave & she turns her head out toward the window. Dead gardens— a glint of color, a blooming orchid somewhere below this black hole in search of more than just darkness.

5

Joaquin Murrieta's head ███ never found. His brain floating in some river, ███ back whipped a hundred times, ███ manhood strangled & cut off. He fought for *mí* ███ *Raza* Power ███ *la Raza Unida*! ███ I walk & stare at ███ wet dirt after ███ rains in *Michoacán Mejico* ███ complicated culture, trying ███ piece together ███ before we were raped, ███ culture lost ███ stolen— a speck of light cutting through green pastures, ███ sun burning dry the hanging *carne de res* soon ███ *carne seca*, ███ the vibrant voices of those *Chicanos y Chicanas* that paved the road ███ Their ghosts haunt me. ███ ███ White America ███ being gay means poverty, being brown ███ being a woman ███ The sky burns blue, the past is dead & gone now ███ I hold ███ breath when I pass ███ cemetery— my breath clamped inside ███ body hiding from ███ spirits who linger-in-between heaven & hell.

6

Love is the color of sky after brushfires engulf hundreds of homes.

    It is the color of hospital gown worn by my *abuelita* waiting to die.
    It is the color of this dark room lit by lighter & cigarette.
El amor es tu mano sobre mis cicatrices.

Love is the color of the sky when not a single bird sings.
Love is the color of aged wine in vintage crystal.

    It is a blackeye because I feel like it.
    It is a condom breaking.
    It is colored bodies on the floor.
    It is shooting those bodies on the floor.
    It is screaming ontop of those bodies on the floor.
El amor es mi lengua dentro de ti.

    It is your lips making a weird shape posing for a #selfie.
    It is the way you suck my dick while driving.
    It is making peanutbutter & jelly naked in the kitchen.
El amor es la lumbre que se traga nuestro hogar.

7

I kneel down & trace my name in the sand with my index finger. There is nothing left in my heart except a few one-night-stands, my brother calling me faggot, my cousin Marilu swallowing pills to kill her baby— someone is waiting for me though, waiting for me to die, to break my bones & drain my veins. They will kiss open my lips & look inside my mouth, searching for dead butterflies and   music.

8

Sometimes I think I'm growing invisible, becoming the color of air, a moth on the wall, the scent of loneliness— yes I know, cliché— becoming just another grain of sand at the bottom of the fuckingocean.

But summers pass seamlessly into winter & my brownskin dries, the brownblood in my veins runs slower than ever, my breath clamped inside my body searches for an escape— seasons passing by, Luis becoming more refined, more feminine   more divine.

9

My grandmother's grandmother was hung on treebranches
by the Texas Rangers when Anglos began to invade my people's land,
began to displace tradition & replace with greed & power—
the AmeriCAN Dream.

Black & brown & yellow don't count in Amerikkka now-a-days:
Afrikanos came singing
Mexicanos came riding
Los Güeros came here shooting,
Indigenous people left crying—
       Decapitated children
       Raped women
       Dragged & gagged
       Hair chopped off
       Homes turned to ashes.

Whose land are we living in?

10

Words die fly like butterflies in my poetry | my language | rhythms hip-hopping through the wind | tick-tocking like clocks | burning like volcanic rock. A flock of birds is a burst of syllables | secrets written as memories turned into dances | movements of the arms & legs & neck snapping up & down. But this *poema* is about song— for the unfound women of *Juárez* | for the crying Mexican babies next door | for the nights my mother went to bed hungry— music fluttering through my bones *como una* migrating *monarca* | flooding tall trees in *Michoacán*.

11

My uncle died at age of 21, shot 6 times for having "East-Side" tattooed on his chest right next to *abuela's* face.   I came out from *mí* mother's womb over-due & drowned in blood the color of theatre curtains— my grandmother named me Luis.   My name means Warrior in English, Famous Warrior in Portuguese, but in Spanish my name only means my dead uncle: His blue eyes long curls side smirks with a cigarette hanging off left lip— drove the *chicas* crazy.   My name means black sheep, lonely & lost looking for a niche that will love the fact that I wear pink, that will open their arms to a man that loves other men, to a *monarca* that flutters from season to season trying to find the next best thing.

12

I am the offspring of the mixed, Indian Spanish blood, the *Mestizo*.
I evolved into *Chicano*, into one of the defeated peoples,
Mejicanos that lost their land to white man, lost their culture to *gringo*
who claims Indigenous land as his own. I am the offspring
who hides behind black branches, the Mexican or greaser, same thing,
that prays to *la Virgencita Morena*, that begs to be heard, prays up to stars
in search of something more than just stereotype, in search of more
than picking red apples hard as knees. I am a mixed mixed man,
a lost face searching for his own *voz*— I hang around now in the dark
belonging to cursed race, looking up to dead beams of light,
making wishes that will never ever come true.

13

Across from her an empty chair, a watered-down Sprite, untouched chips'n'salsa. To the left & right, twenty more chairs. ██████████████ ███████████████████████████████ nothing sweet about it. God stopped listening a while back, so prayer was out of the question. ██████████ ██████ love ██████████████████████████

She sat alone, numb to the screeching sounds the forks & knives made against white plates, ████████████████ text-messages: ██████████ ████████████████████████████████████ — stale chips crushed between her teeth, the faint taste of ~~salsa~~ hate numbing her lips.

14

There is nothing   left in *mí*.

15

Asphalt slips into the cracks of my Nikes, running in June
breath begins to dry parched like the Mojave Desert &
the Sycamores float above *mí*, tiny birds looking down
singing unknown melodies to *mí*, serenading *mí* down
an endless path—the blue sky filled with clouds &
you can never have too much
                                                    sky

16

From the day we were born we heard gunshots. My mother yelling at us
to go hide in the closet, my father passed out still drunk from the night before,
a scream from the front door— my neighbor shot in the chest three times,
his mother raped, his dog kicked to death & it was only Monday.
Gay brown boi still weeps.

17

The *guayabo* trees in Mexico always had something to give, a delicate fragrance, white & pink insides, green leaves & small white flowers for tea. My grandfather used to cut *guayabas* in half, dip them in goat milk & drizzle honey over them. They were better than chocolate. He would die the following year a week before my birthday. 1995. April. I remember. I was ten.

But mourning will ripen with time like fruit falling from trees & the *guayabas* will keep tasting the same, year after year,

goat milk or not.

18

I will die in this *casa*. Rustic bookshelves drown the walls, my poetry hidden within the pages of old magazines & reviews & newspapers & books dance articles here & there; body won't be found for a week!

My body will stink of cats & piss, the ants & flies feasting on the past. I will stop answering phone calls after my husband's death, trapping myself within four walls, hoarding memories tragedies anything that reminds me of ~~Carlos~~ him.

I will try & fail many times drinking many nights more than several painkillers, cutting my wrists & even learning how to pray once again; I will pray to die. Will pray to *Nuestra Señora de los Dolores.* To have my soul set free. My body left to rot.

Spider webs will connect the bookshelves to the kitchen,

the kitchen to the fireplace &

the fireplace to the bathroom,

where my body will be found: half smashed face, crushed knees, a gold *rosario* threaded between my fingers.

19

Dust collects beneath my bed. Small clumps of linen & hair & dead
skin sit on top of my hookah & old wall décor. I sweep these floors with
mom's old *escoba*, clean the mirrors with an old pair of my bikini briefs,
take down the crosses hung on mint walls:
Packing. Moving. Migrating.   This brown boi butterfly

twitches: He is ready to rip open from cocoon.

20

Everyone in my family has different eyes. My handicapped father the color of water, sometimes blue, sometimes green | my tired mother has my grandmother's eyes, a burned cinnamon, years of cooking & cleaning you can see right through them | my homophobic brother a pale brown, like emptiness, nothing moves in there, he looks left, he looks right | my divorced sister, wide & the shade of cherry wood or with makeup, a darker wood, her eyelashes hiding fear & disappointment | my unhappy sister, the housewife, her eyes a sweet honey, large & full of regret, the most submissive of us all.

My eyes are black, mysterious holes, see beauty in the tiniest of things, a crack on the sidewalk, the pollen inside a flower, black & dark like an old woman's veil, dark brown like the dirt my grandmother was buried in last year, black like the early morning. Everyone in my family has the same light skin tone, has the same curly hair, has the same traditions…

but me.

21

Ruby red my lover said. The color of his father's guitar
has replaced father'n'son time. We don't mention his name
around here. When he makes love to *mí* his long eyelashes
& dark eyes remind *mí* of priest *padre* father *Ruben*. He came
in *mí* when I was six. Told *mí* it was ok   it would feel good.

But now our bodies one on top of the other sweat to forget
the wounds that keep opening: When will I stop   feeling
Father, your hands bruising my waist.

22

Crooked bodies walk sidebyside in search of the river turned   silk. No luck.
Chrysanthemum eyes chamomile lips, face down upsidedown, smiles of honey
& lavender, coconut & pineapple. Nor skin or bone or wax or soap
can hear the clicking ticking sound a soul makes when it escapes.

Let me start over: here I am in South Bend and the only thing I think about
is how many fucking crucifixes are hung on the white walls of white Notre Dame.
The white sky is doubled.   I can't see straight.

23

How do you deal with bloodonblood & how do you stop from cutting balls off? He raped her. Once a week. For many years. She was 11. He was future graduate from ███████ University. Psychologist. ██████████ *Mi sangre*. BloodinBlood.

24

Words slip from tongues around *mí* lingering through my intestines,
suffocating *mí*   haunting mí. My heart goes thump thump numb.
Their fingers point: It pierces through my brownflesh &
continues to the next victim. Colored glittered bodies on display. Media
controls us like streetlights:
Go, Stop, No!

                   Those tongues

                will not

                                 prevail.

25

Brown gay boi eats from brown-bag lunch & white people don't know how to react, his earrings dangling down to his broad shoulders, his Raybans, black Mexican beard, the *Walter Mercado* style essence jewelry he wears slays displays: Jealous butterflies floating up into the blue, an invisible I hate you, his nipples sore from the night before.

26

They stop me at airports after I pass inspection, ask me to put my hands out & spread. The run a gun up&down my brown body betting I have something on *mí, pero no tengo nada cabrones!* Arizona officers nod, they stop on my crotch, I smile & they let me pass. I grab my shit & with that frozen smile I walk like a profiled styled model. Adidas against floor. Diamond earrings on earlobe. White plane white ticket:

going home.

27

You instruct *mí* to open you up like a Christmas gift, unwrapping your *moño* bow, splitting open your walls, your box, sticking my face in the inside of heaven. My *dedos* fingers draw a tiny globe around your nipples, no assembly required. Your teeth leave dents on my forearms, hickies spreading on my back like a flight of geese. Your erection, hard then soft, tickles *mí, me gusta,* reminds *mí* of church: our eyes gazing feasting dreaming screaming of orgy-filled nights flights...
Like tonight. Like last night.   Like tomorrow night.

28

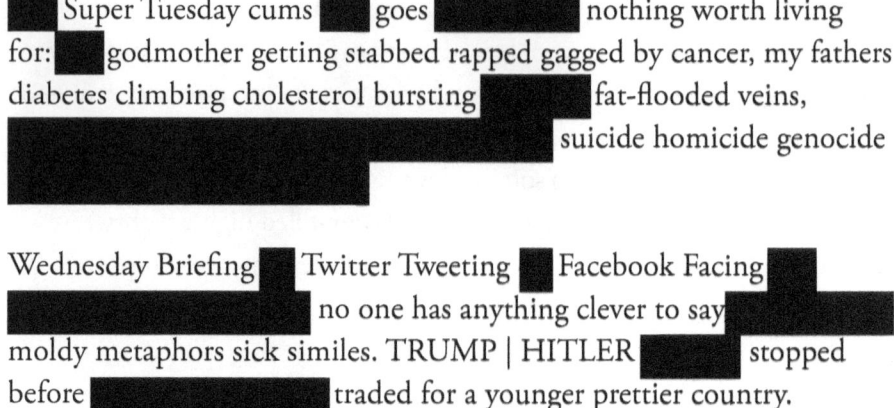

■ Super Tuesday cums ■ goes ■ nothing worth living
for: ■ godmother getting stabbed rapped gagged by cancer, my fathers
diabetes climbing cholesterol bursting■ fat-flooded veins,
suicide homicide genocide

Wednesday Briefing■ Twitter Tweeting ■ Facebook Facing■
no one has anything clever to say■
moldy metaphors sick similes. TRUMP | HITLER■ stopped
before ■ traded for a younger prettier country.

29

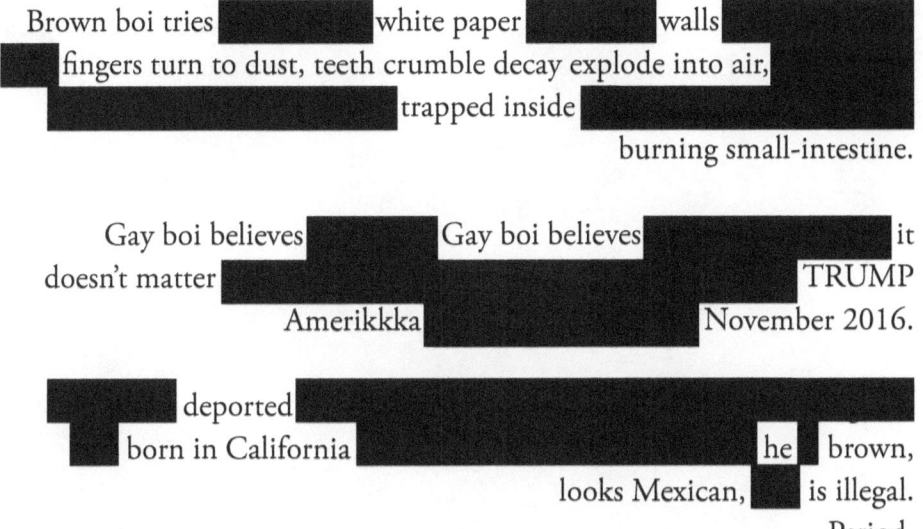

Brown boi tries ███████ white paper ████████ walls ███
███ fingers turn to dust, teeth crumble decay explode into air, ███
trapped inside ████████
burning small-intestine.

Gay boi believes ████████ Gay boi believes ████████ it
doesn't matter ████████████ TRUMP
Amerikkka November 2016.

███████ deported ████████████████
born in California ████████████████ he brown,
looks Mexican, ███ is illegal.
Period.

30

Water cascading & rumbling rumbling   rumbling, my cock shriveling in cold water: nothing here to see, nothing here to hear, nothing here to eat.

31

But everything is cold to me now. My *mamá* used to say we all killed Jesus, but I'm starting to believe

he is still

alive.

About the Author

LUIS LOPEZ-MALDONADO is a Xicanx activist, poeta, playwright, dancer, choreographer, and educator born and raised in multiple barrios across el Orange County, CA. He/Him/They/Them are authors of *Mexican Bird*, from Querencia Press. They earned a Bachelor of Arts degree from the University of California Riverside, in Creative Writing and Dance. His/Their poetry has been seen in *The American Poetry Review, Foglifter, Public Pool,* and *Latina Outsiders: Remaking Latina Identity,* among many others. He/They also earned a Master of Arts degree in Dance from Florida State University and a Master of Fine Arts degree in Creative Writing from the University of Notre Dame. He/They are currently adding glitter to the Land of Enchantment, working for the public educational system as a high school Bilingual Educator and Special Education Teacher. He/They are currently a graduate student at the University of New Mexico, to become an educational administrator.

FLOWERSONG
PRESS

FlowerSong Press nurtures essential verse from, about, and throughout the borderlands. Literary. Lyrical. Boundless.

Sign up for announcements about
new and upcoming titles at:

www.flowersongpress.com

www.ingramcontent.com/pod-product-compliance
Lightning Source LLC
Chambersburg PA
CBHW030915140626
46545CB00017B/2364